PAINT BY STICKER

KIDS

HOLLY JOLLY CHRISTMAS

workman

• NEW YORK •

Library of Congress Cataloging-in-Publication Data is available.

ISBN 978-1-5235-1856-2

Design by Ying Cheng

The 10 low-poly images in this book are based on illustrations by Ying Cheng.

Workman books are available at special discounts when purchased in bulk for premiums and sales promotions as well as for fundraising or educational use. Special editions or book excerpts can also be created to specification. For details, contact the Special Sales Director at specialmarkets@workman.com.

Workman Publishing Co., Inc.
225 Varick Street
New York, NY 10014-4381

workman.com

WORKMAN and PAINT BY STICKER are registered trademarks of Workman Publishing Co., Inc.

Printed in China

First printing September 2022

10 9 8 7 6 5 4 3 2 1

HOW TO PAINT BY STICKER

STICKER MAP

STICKER SHEET

56

1. PICK YOUR IMAGE. Sticker maps for each image are in the front of the book. Do you want to sticker the twinkling Christmas tree or the jolly puppy? It's up to you!

2. FIND YOUR STICKERS. Sticker sheets for each image are in the back of the book. Use the picture in the top right corner of each sticker sheet to find the one that goes with your image. Both the sticker sheet and the sticker map can be torn out of the book, so you don't have to flip back and forth between them.

3. MATCH THE NUMBERS. Each sticker has a number that matches a space on the sticker map. Place each sticker in the space on the sticker map with the matching number. Be careful! The stickers aren't removable.

4. WATCH YOUR PAINTING COME TO LIFE! After you've finished your masterpiece, you can frame it, use it as decoration, or give it as a gift.

ARE YOU READY? LET'S START STICKERING!

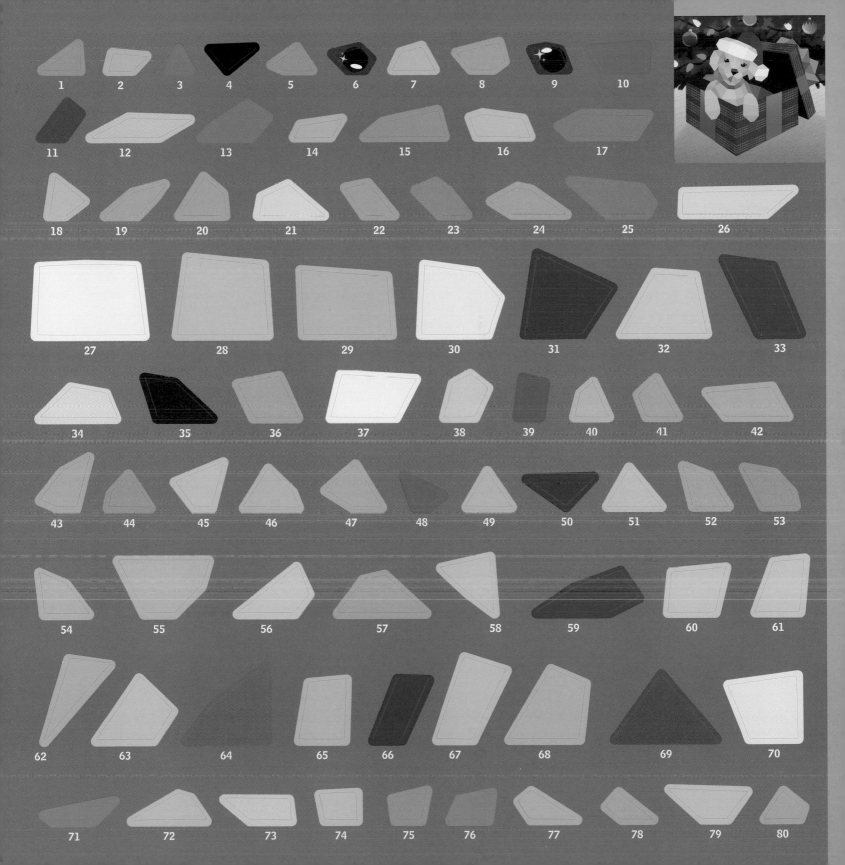

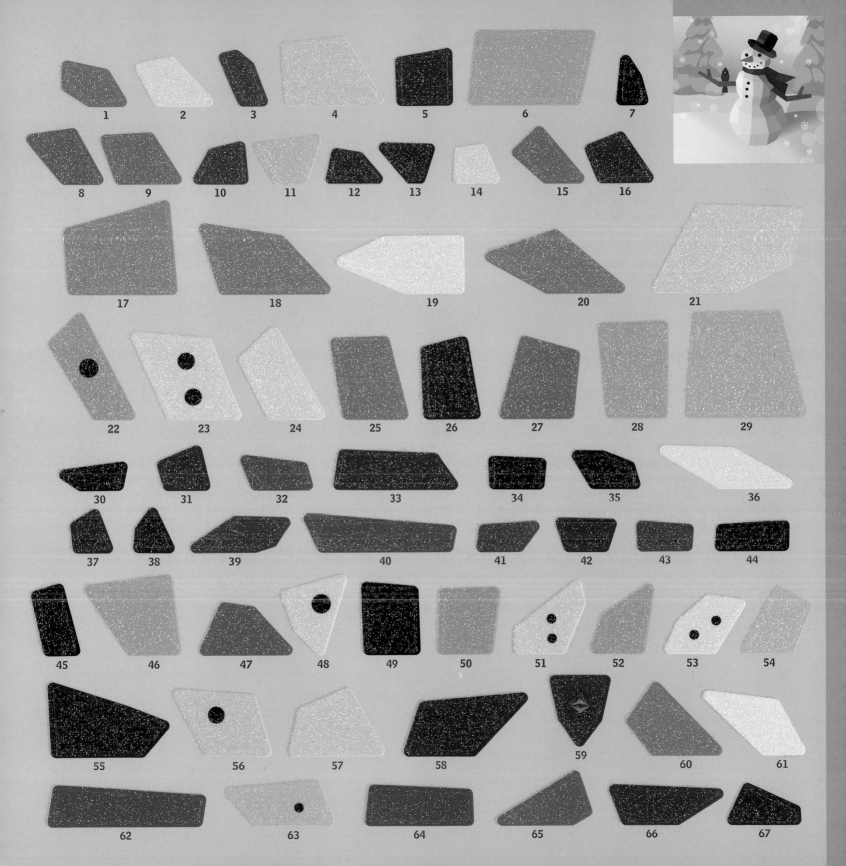

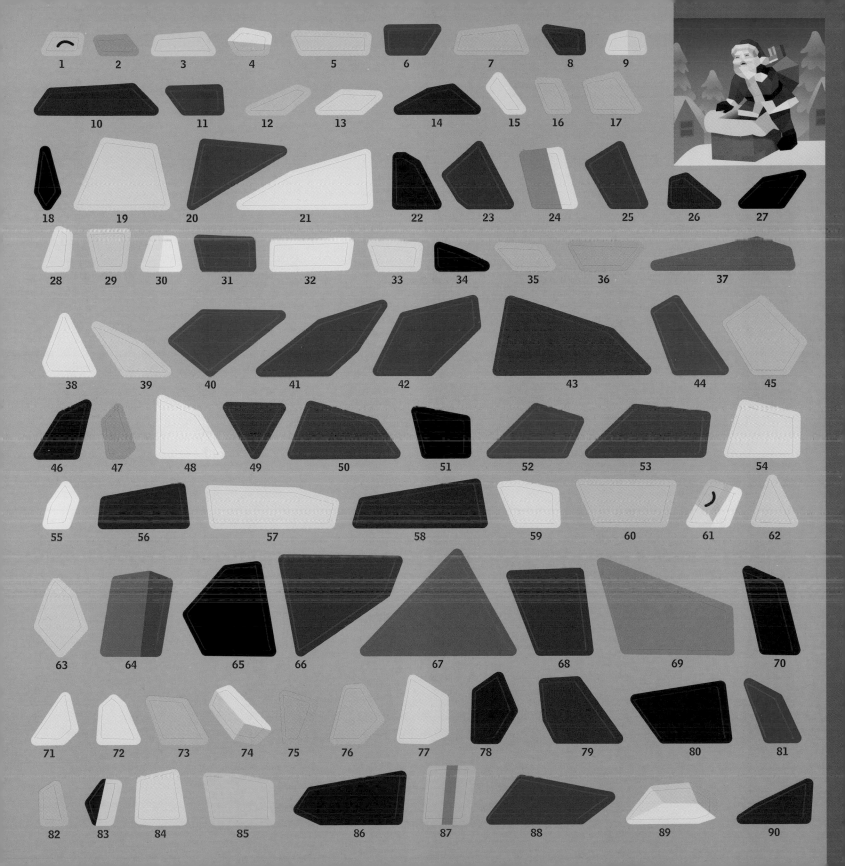

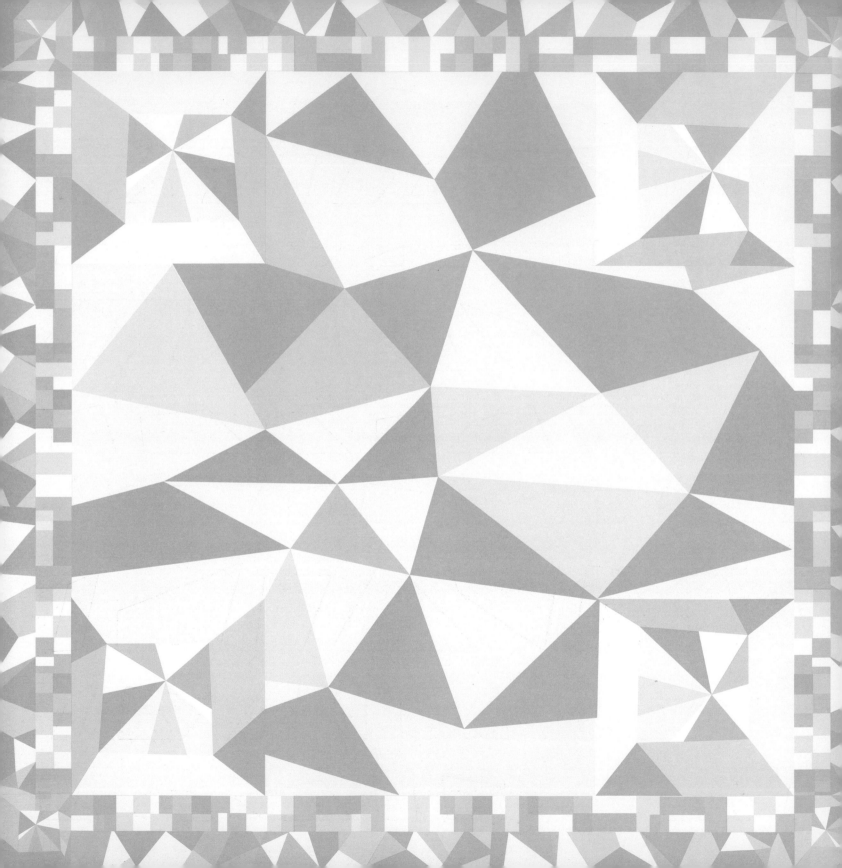

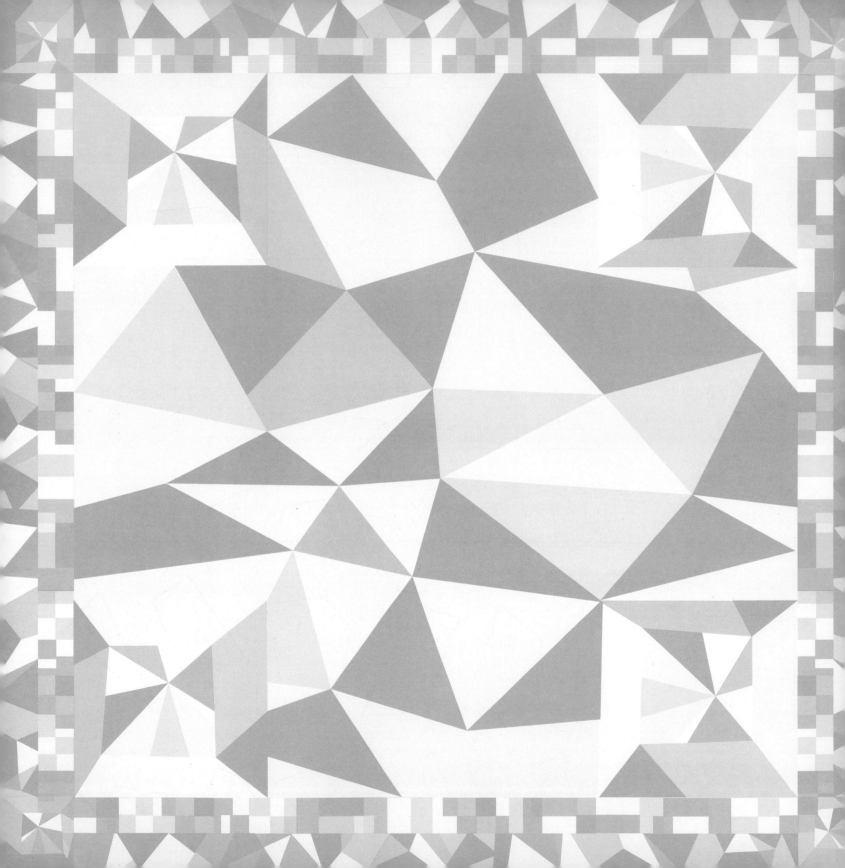

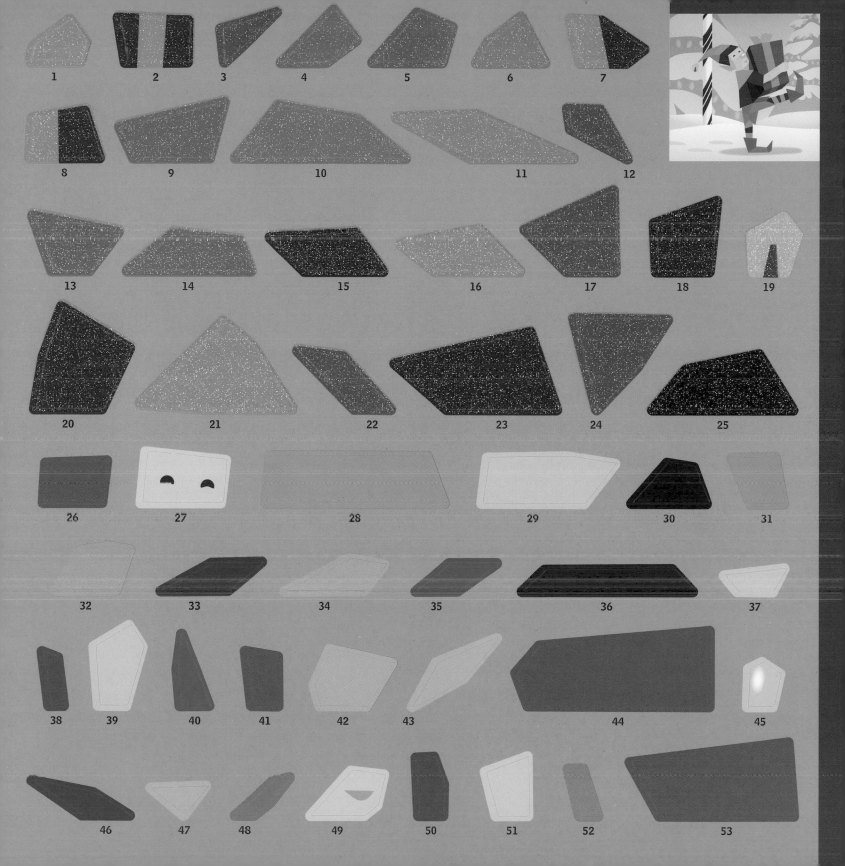

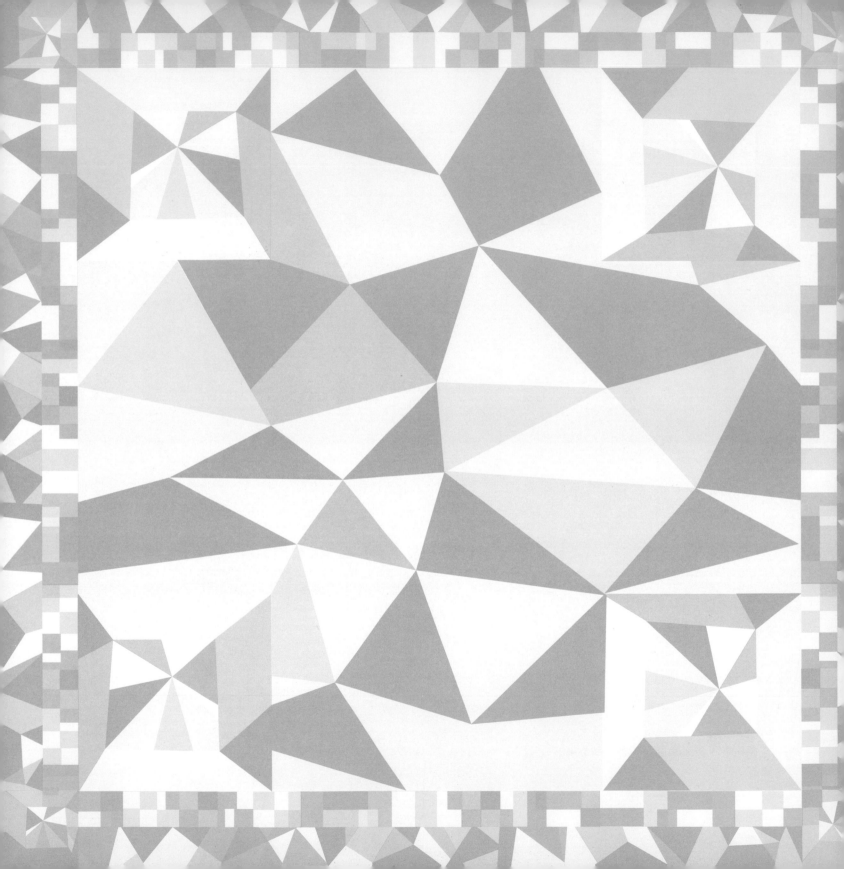

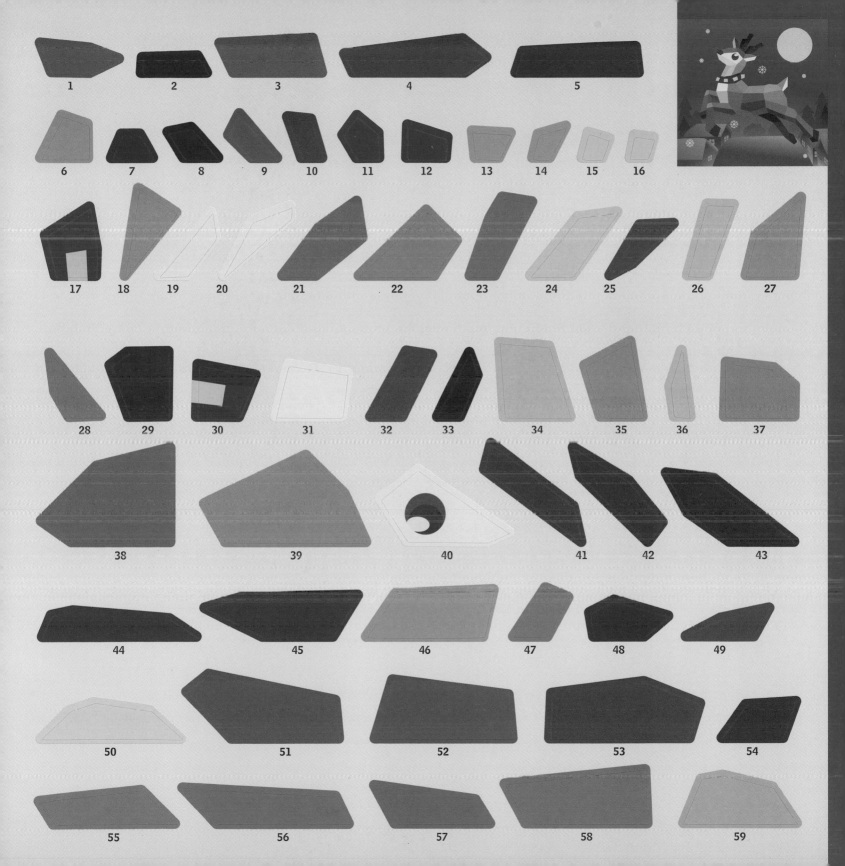

1

2

3

4

5

6

7

8

9

10

11

12

13

14

15

16

17

18

19

20

21

22

23

24

25

26

27

28

29

30

31

32

33

34

35

36

37

38

39

40

41

42

43

44

45

46

47

48

49

50

51

52

53

54

55

56

57

58

59

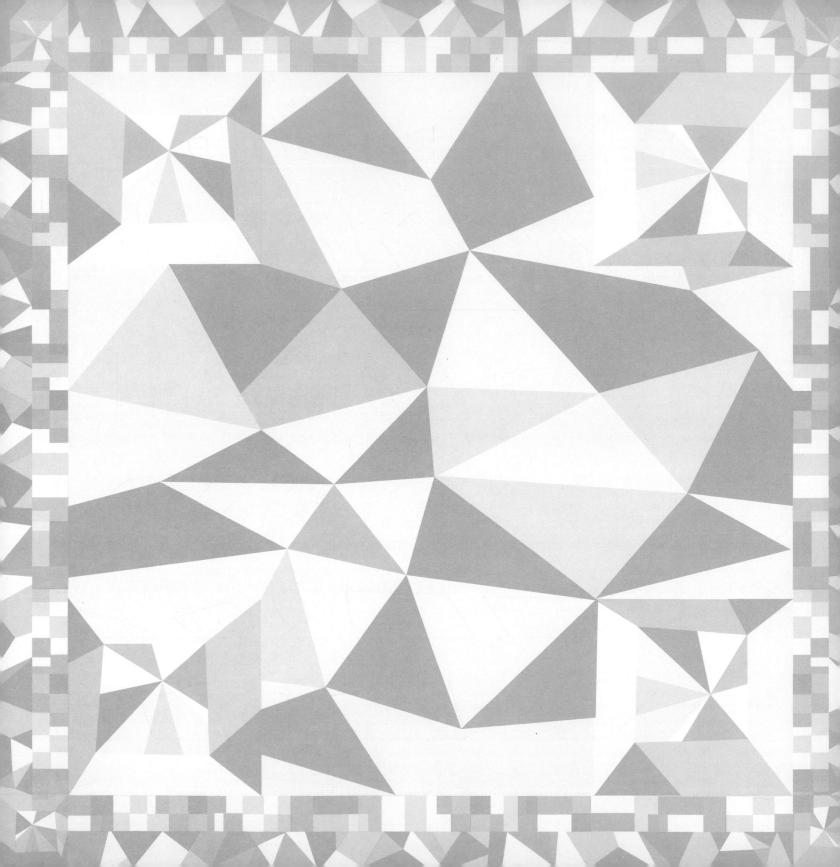

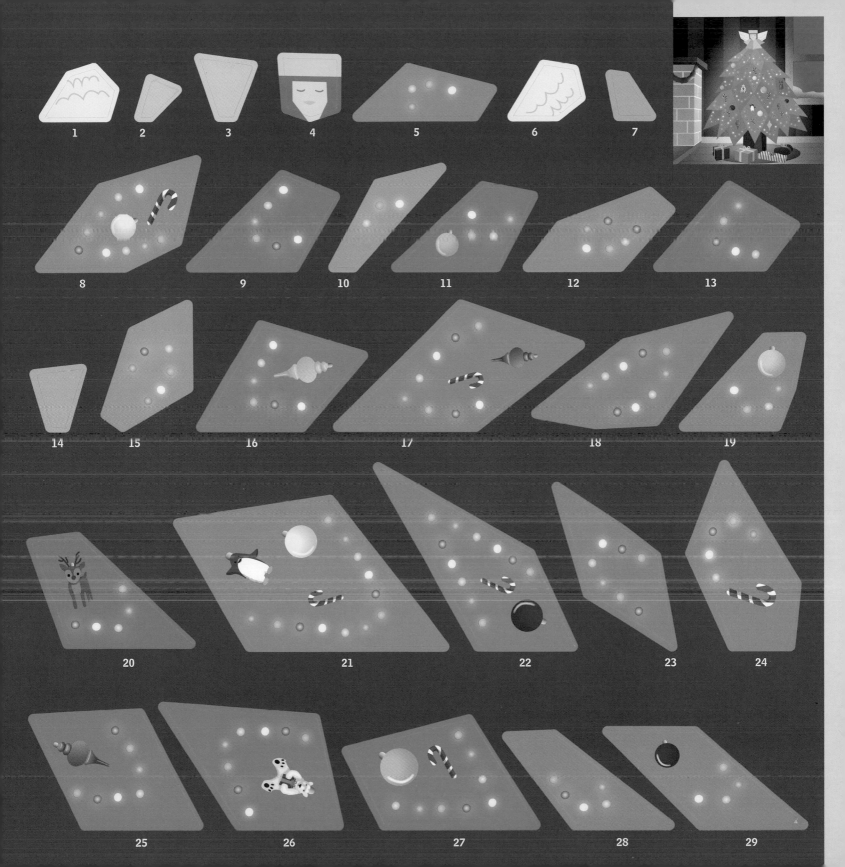

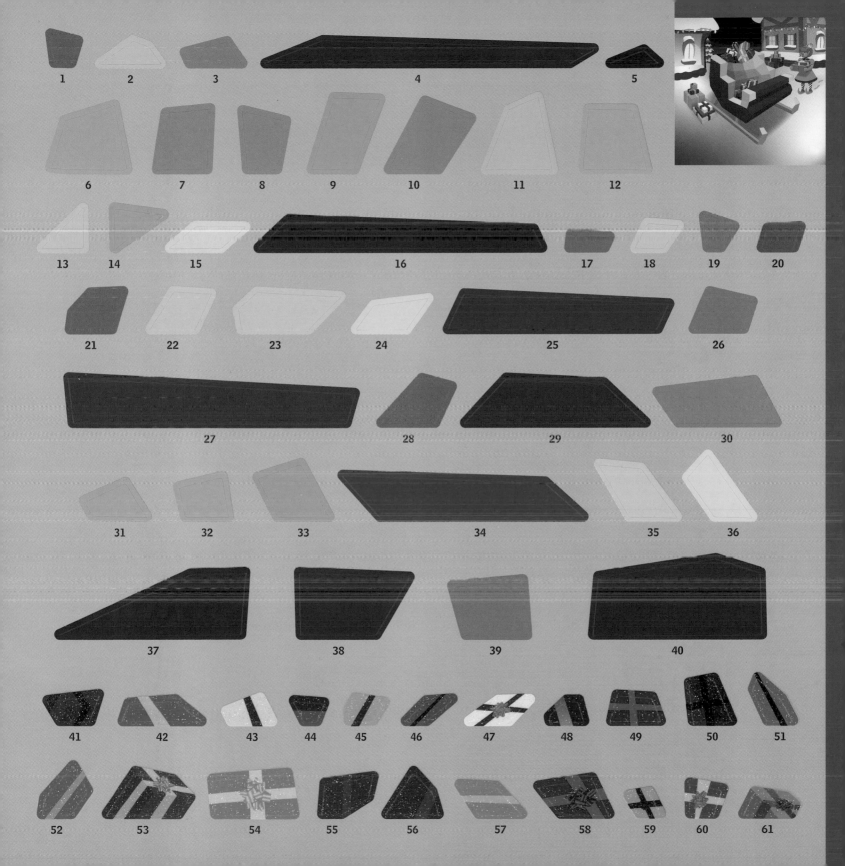

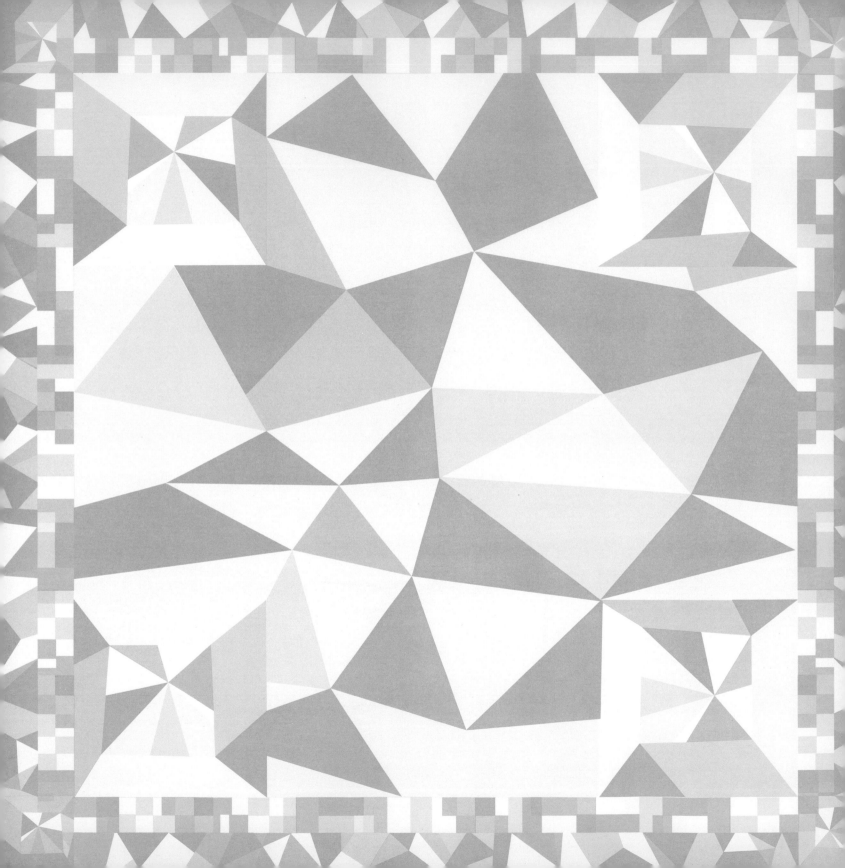

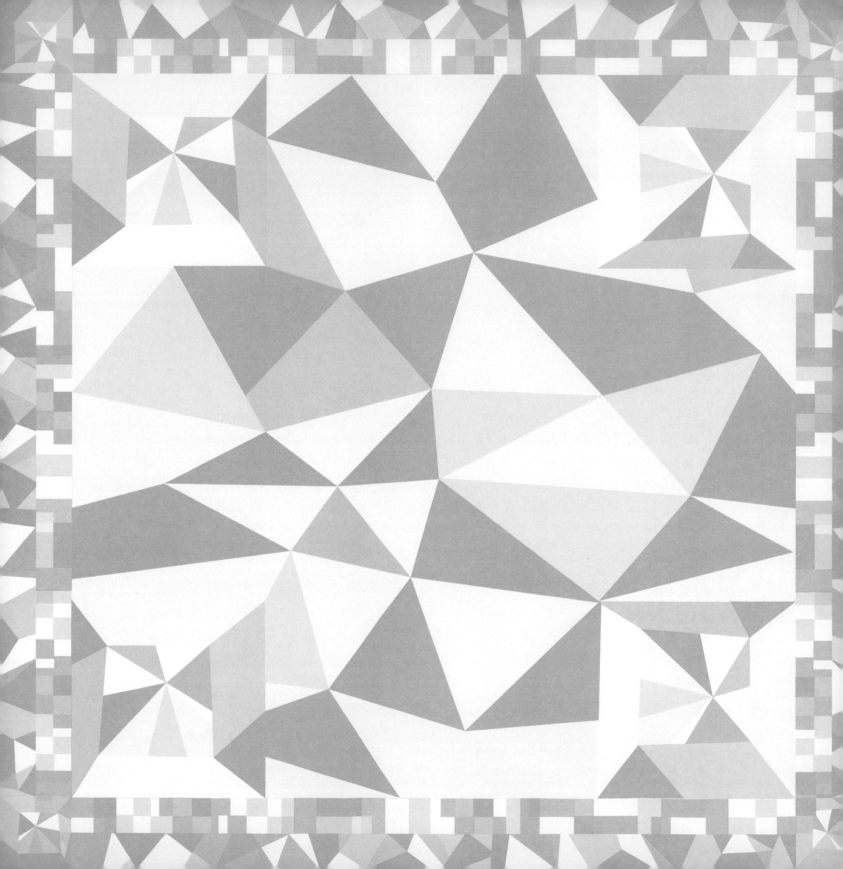